THE PANDEMIC AND ME

LAURA LAVAYÉN

The Pandemic and Me
Copyright © 2024 by Laura Lavayén

ISBN: 978-1639458295 (sc)
ISBN: 978-1639459391 (hc)
ISBN: 978-1639458301 (e)

All rights reserved. No part of this publication may be reproduced, distributed, or transmitted in any form or by any means, including photocopying, recording, or other electronic or mechanical methods, without the prior written permission of the publisher, except in the case brief quotations embodied in critical reviews and other noncommercial uses permitted by copyright law.

The views expressed in this book are solely those of the author and do not necessarily reflect the views of the publisher, and the publisher hereby disclaims any responsibility for them.

Writers' Branding
(877) 608-6550
www.writersbranding.com
media@writersbranding.com

CONTENTS

Chapter 1 1

Chapter 2 5

Chapter 3 9

Chapter 4 19

Chapter 5 29

Chapter 6 37

Chapter 7 45

CHAPTER 1

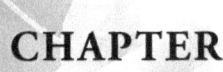

Today I am trying to write about the problems that living in a time of pandemic caused me. I think the first time I heard about the pandemic was when it had just started and what I heard was that it was a virus that had been born in China. I said to myself that China was too far away for it to reach Argentina, the country where I was born and which I always visit from January to March every year. I was on vacation and I did not plan to spend a long time worrying about something that seemed to be so far away.

My sister Silvia who traveled with me was visiting a sister who lives in the city of Roca and arrived with the news that she only had two days to leave Argentina and leave the country before the international flights were suspended. I told her no… She came after me and told me that she would travel the next day. I told her that I would not go with her because I had a ticket to travel in two days. She told me again that she would leave because the airports were going to close and then she would not be able to leave. I told her that I would not leave until the day I had my ticket. The next day she left for the airport and told me that she hoped I would leave too because if not, I would not be able to travel. The next day Silvia left and I went out to confirm my ticket. To my surprise I found out that the office was closed and I went back to my other sister's house where I was staying and found my brother coming back from the airport. Amazed he told me that Silvia had gotten lucky and had told him to tell me to go confirm my ticket at the airport and he would take me right away. He took me to the airport which was full of passengers wanting to leave.

The purpose of traveling on an airline from my country is that the plane to Bariloche leaves from there. If I take another airline I cannot make the transfer from Buenos Aires to Bariloche because I would have to go to the airport. This way the connection is easier. I was proved right, but by the next day I felt tired and was beginning to regret not having listened to my sister and traveled with her. Because there was a world of passengers trying to figure out where they should go. The airport had become a place where everyone was running around trying to find where their plane was leaving from. But I was following those who seemed to know where my plane was leaving from because I heard it would still make it to Kennedy Airport without a problem.

The trip was very tiring, we were asked to show our documents several times. Once in the seat of the plane I was surprised to see that it was not as full of passengers as I thought. But tired and all, I breathed a sigh of relief when we landed at Kennedy airport. With horror I saw that the place where the cabs were located was empty. I saw a man with a sign offering to take me anywhere. He gave me a huge price to take me to Philadelphia and when I said it was too much he offered me a discount and I had to accept.

Back home I started to put the correspondence in order and I saw that there were many things waiting for me to sort out. First, I had to get the bills in order to pay the expenses of the

light and other things. Thanks to Silvia I didn't have to go out and buy a mask to cover my mouth because she had prepared everything for me to go as soon as possible to do other things I would need. The few people I met already had their mouths covered. Everyone seemed to want to get things done that day. I looked at the people on the street and it even seemed to me that they were walking as if shooting at each other. But I still had to listen more to the news to understand that we were in a difficult situation. Until then I didn't understand whether what I was experiencing had to do with the Chinese or not. I didn't understand what was going on and I remembered a movie of a situation that I thought was more or less like that. But, little by little, I began to understand that the situation we were in was complex.

I also began to understand that we were living moments we had never lived before. When I got home I had an altercation with Silvia because I thought it was exaggerated that she would not let me put my hand to my nose, not even to wipe it. In the end I lost my patience and yelled at her that if she wanted to be mortified for fear of contagion I was going to take care of myself as much as possible too but not so exaggeratedly. She got angry and went to where she lives. I decided that I would take care of myself as much as possible, but I didn't want to do it to the point that my nerves would attack me every time I saw someone who wasn't wearing a mask. I tried not to overdo it, but slowly I began to think that nothing seemed to be that serious. I isolated myself from everyone. Just when I thought I could write a book about what I was going through I realized that what I was going through I couldn't call life. And it even seemed to me that it was all a nightmare. I remembered that many times in my life I lived something similar, for different reasons. But the moments when I was so lonely come to my memory, but I think it was for something different. Maybe because I didn't experience those moments of loneliness in the same way or because it was a different time. I was young. But I think it is late for me to remember what wants to come back to my memory and it doesn't come because I don't know what I want to remember. I think now that I don't know what could have happened to me, maybe it would be something connected with illness. I came to think that I didn't want to remember what wants to come to my memory because it was something that hurt me or I know it will bring bad memories to my mind and fear of getting sick. We were not to make mistakes by not following the rules of taking care of ourselves. Rules that all made me assume that I should not get close to anyone because we did not know if that person was infected, but I still do not know if I felt sick. Everything scared me, even though I tried to think that itching in my nose was driving me crazy.

Every time Silvia saw me holding my hand anywhere on my face she would scream and stomp her feet in rage. I started to fight with her. I thought she wouldn't go where she worked because she didn't want to travel. I immediately saw that one way to catch it was to travel on public transportation. When she told me that she would not come back to visit me until she was sure that the danger had passed, she left without a second thought. For me, everything got complicated. I looked for ways to try to learn to live alone. It was more difficult on weekends because since I left my rural home in Argentina to go to work in Buenos Aires she always followed me. And we were never far from each other.

The first few months seemed endless. But I tried to get my life in order. I entertained myself by reading some books by authors I had owned for a long time. And I sang alone to the beat of some record I hadn't listened to since a record player I owned broke. No neighbor complained. Everything was the same for me. But the day came when they started to give the vaccine against the virus that began to kill without mercy. It was unbelievable what was happening, I was starting to get scared and I was afraid of being one of the victims. But I could not manage to get the vaccine. However, I didn't give up and in the end, I don't know how I managed it, when they told me that there was a place to get it in a pharmacy I decided to go to the one near my house. They told me they didn't have Moderna, which was the one I wanted. I decided to accept the one they had told me they would put me in right away. I couldn't believe it when they gave me an appointment for the next day. When they finally vaccinated me, I breathed again knowing that, with the vaccine, even if I got the virus, it would not be so deadly.

I felt sure that, by getting vaccinated, I would not catch it. Many thought that whoever would get it, would get it. Many people had to die to make everyone follow the rules. The most important of all was to get vaccinated and wear a mask and keep your distance.

CHAPTER 2

I felt like a prisoner. If I wanted to watch television to calm down, it was impossible. Because instead of hearing that we were united to defeat an evil more terrible than a war, we found that the media spent more time showing the worst of human beings. In Philadelphia there was and still is more than one crime per day. I don't think more people died from the virus than died in the protests that are still going on. These protests were protesting, but they opened a door to contagion.   Sometimes the protests were peaceful. At other times the crowds could spread and it was dangerous the evil that could be caused if among the people gathered some would be carriers of the virus. No one would breathe a sigh of relief again until there was not one person left who had not been vaccinated so that we could be sure we were free of the contagion.

My grandmother told me that when she was young there was a plague of tuberculosis and she and her mother, whenever there was danger of contagion, went to help the neighbors. So she told me that she also covered her mouth with a chinstrap and that is how she treated several neighbors and cured them. Remembering my grandmother, I think she protected herself to the maximum. I remember her telling me that they used alcohol as a disinfectant and other home remedies. Surely it was a plant because she knew how to give us some juices. She also knew which were the healing plants for each illness. They were plants that she dried in the sun. As much as I liked to cure myself, I would only tell her that I felt bad when I had a cold because she would give me a spoonful of olive oil followed by a spoonful of honey. Since I rarely got sick, and grandma kept the honey she bought in big canning jars, sometimes I would pretend to be sick and take a spoonful on an empty stomach. For stomach aches it was mint that grew near a stream and we would take it with pure bee honey. She told me that, in her youth, her mother accustomed her to eat slowly and when we would visit her friends' house she would give me lessons on how we should sit at the table and eat in moderation.

In this time of pandemic I remember what my life was like at my grandmother's house, which I remember with much love. All the time I have not been going out much, I think that I am going through a time of trial where I am resigned to whatever I have to live every day. I feel like I did when I was a child, with that anxiety as if I wanted to fly and my wings were broken. Sometimes it seems to me that I will never feel sure of myself. I had started to think that I no longer wanted to do anything I had dreamed of... I thought about living a more peaceful life, enjoying what I have and not getting involved in things that require a lot of work. I don't have my ambitions anymore.

Now I just think this is going to be the last time I write a biography of myself. But I don't know why I like to get into things that are so hard for me to do. Anyway, it must be my ambition or something that makes me always worried. Sometimes I talk to myself and say: "Laura, why don't you live quietly the time you have left; travel, go to your homeland, enjoy being with your family. But I think about it and suddenly it is as if I had something or someone telling me: "live the life that touches you, stop weaving fantasies of things that are not for you". But there is no case, I always go back to look for new adventures. Don't get ahead of the future, let things go as they should. But I always go back to imagine something. And that leads me to think that, if God sent us this pandemic to make us reason and try to be better and behave like human beings, I think he was wrong. There were more congregations and protest meetings. One

I remember was the one they did when George Floyd was killed by the police, it made me feel so bad. I don't think a man should have to be beaten and treated that way. I remember seeing it on the news on TV and then in the papers. The news went international. I still seem to see the man begging to be allowed to breathe. I never understood why they took him prisoner, the way I saw him on the ground and the policeman who was choking him... sometimes it seemed to me that it was all a figment of my imagination, but they showed it once and I don't know how many more times.

It seemed so terrible to me when I saw the amount of people in a protest that it was fair but it was not the right time to do it. So there continued to be conglomerations of people when they should have been isolated as it was a way to avoid contagion. And the months passed, I was sure that even then we would not be free of contagion. I resigned myself to continue waiting for them to say that everything was going to get better.

LAURA LAVAYÉN

CHAPTER

3

Months went by and I lived to dream and imagine that everything was going to be all right before January because I lived waiting for that month since every year I thought I would go to visit my family in Argentina. I don't know if there was any news about the end of the pandemic. But that did not happen and I wanted to go on thinking that in January we could go back to our old life. But I was wrong and a year passed and nothing had changed. The contagion was still going on. They kept telling people that they shouldn't be in groups of many because the contagion continued. It was impossible to get them to listen. They would group together on holidays or do protests, they would travel…they looked like wayward kids ready to get their own way.

But, to my misfortune, there was talk of a new virus and it was said to be more fierce than the Corona 19 virus. The fear only calmed down a little when there was another vaccine and they thought you would be completely out of danger. I trembled when I watched the news and heard about other crimes. I don't know how people still dared to go out on the streets. Every night more than one person died. It was no longer the burglar who broke into a house to steal, this time it was killers who looked like children playing at being a Wild West gunslinger. For them it seemed like a game to bet with a revolver on who was better. The human being had lost his humanity and did not care about anything.

Everyone heard about what was happening on the news. I remember it seemed so inhumane the first time there was a school robbery. I never thought that would happen again. I felt chills every time it happened again and again. But what I find most difficult to ascertain is how or why guns still can't be wiped off the earth, how they have remained within everyone's reach. It is that the human being is getting so selfish and is losing the sense of humanity to such an extent that it gives them pleasure to kill just because, no more. I think that reminds us that the history of man begins with the first crime, when one of the firstborn of Adam and Eve killed his brother.

In the history of all times we see that we have not changed much and as long as we continue to manufacture weapons, wars and other problems that this causes us will not cease. To watch a newscast we must be brave because they are becoming more and more violent. I already say when I go to turn on the TV: "let's see what bad news there is". When I say this they usually tell me: "that will never change."

I never felt so bad about not being able to go visit my family. I still didn't visit my acquaintances often. And I lived waiting because I always went to Argentina in January since it is summer there and I suffer a lot when it is cold because I have arthritis and mine is the one that makes me suffer when it is cold. The truth is that I had a bad winter. I even thought that one day I would not be able to walk anymore. But I tried to hold on.

Spring arrived and I started to prepare to go to Bariloche, my hometown.

I was born. The pandemic had made me suffer enough and I was sure that it was not going to fail me again. I kept trying to hold on and not get carried away by the insecurity I was experiencing. The days continued to pass slowly. I felt like I did when I was a child living with a relative so I could go to school and go home on vacation. Like then, I lived trying to make the days go by fast. But they seemed to move at a slow pace. And each thing that came to my mind made me feel better. One day I wanted to write about what we were going through, but I felt so empty that I didn't even want to try.

I couldn't believe that I had to spend another year depriving myself of so many things… not going to the Senior Activity Center where I went almost every day to exercise, dance and sometimes I even got up the courage to sing. Something I like to do because I believe that when I am alone I can do it, however, if I have to do it in public I get out of breath and I am afraid that I will forget the lyrics of the songs or since I have to do it in English it is even worse. Anyway, I tell myself, "I'm not at the Colón in Buenos Aires, nor at the opera in New York." I was shy because when I was a girl I was always criticized by my relatives because they said I didn't do it well. But now that I'm away from them I act brave and, good or bad, I sing. My poor neighbors must hate me because I have those days when I feel like Libertad Lamarque, an Argentine singer who was very famous, she was my father's favorite, and I wear myself out singing. With a sad tango or a happy song when I'm happy. And why not a song by Sinatra or Doris Day. The important thing is to let off steam or rejoice by singing, not to be overcome by the problems that are never lacking. Going back to the year 2021, I have to make an effort to remember, because I lived many days, weeks and months leading such a monotonous life and with so little to remember that I prefer not to try to do it because those days were for me as if I had not lived them.

I wanted to write another novel, but it was as if I had an empty mind, I couldn't think of anything. The worst was the winter. I don't remember if it snowed. But I remember that the colder the day got, the more my legs hurt to the point that I could hardly get up. I insisted on doing it because it seemed to me that if I let myself be it would be worse. Little by little I calmed down. Since my husband passed away I have been losing my memory a little bit, but I think that if I still have something left it is because I make an effort and try to remember what I can't bring to my mind, because I have found a way to do it by not leaving or conforming myself when in the middle of a conversation I suddenly don't remember what I was talking about. But I tried many ways to remember. And I'm getting better and better. I was never going to think I would go a day without having to forget what I was talking about.

I consulted a doctor who told me that it happened to all of us sooner or later. So I decided to find a way not to have a bad time while talking to someone. I told myself that what was happening to me was that I was getting nervous and I learned to calm down and not take life as much trouble. It can still happen to me that my mind goes blank, but I continue with my system of not letting myself be defeated and trying to make an effort so that my mind does not go blank. I went back to reading some phrases or poems and repeating them ad nauseam. First reading it out loud. Then writing phrases or poems and repeating them, first out loud and then reading them, then writing them down, closing the notebook and trying to record them in my mind.

So I went through the year 2021 and I was getting closer to 2022. I thought I would not make a problem for myself and start preparing to go to Argentina. I felt sure that in 2022 we were going to feel safe again and I ignored when they started to talk again that another virus was coming and it was more contagious than COVID-19. But I ignored it. I already had the second vaccination and I felt confident that I would be able to travel to my country without any problem. I had been going every year for a long time and luck could not treat me like that. Many people told me that there was already talk of another virus that was stronger than the current pandemic. But I kept thinking that it would not happen and I started to prepare myself to travel in January.

Two years ago I had left some books at a printer's to put them in the bookstores of Bariloche. I had been publishing books for many years without any ambition that they would be welcomed. But one day I found myself thinking that in my life I had always struggled so hard to make some of my dreams come true and I never succeeded... because I could never carry my ambitions to the end. I have written about ten books and never even succeeded with some of them. Nothing happened beyond being told I wrote well. But suddenly I feel like I deserve some praise. Some people have liked my books and they say there is something for everyone. Now I leave them in the hands of destiny. May it be what God wills. I hope that not everything ends up as money blown away by the wind.

I ask God to help me and before he takes me away he will give me just one of the many favors I have asked for. It must be that since I am always asking him for something I have tired him and it is over for me to fulfill some of my crazy wishes. Then, anyway, I don't think I've been a bad person... maybe I don't deserve anything or I ask for too much? In the end, of all the works I have done in this world I don't think I ever had the strength and patience to carry my dreams to the end. Every time I wanted to do something I fell by the wayside. It must be because I wanted to fly too high and I am afraid of heights.

Today I feel as if the world has come crashing down on me. I try to remember what else happened in 2021. But nothing comes to my memory, I am already approaching the time when I will get the tickets to travel. I remember that everything seemed to be against me. Around Christmas I remember I wanted to have a get-together with some friends. And everything was a failure. I went on December 24 to the supermarket and I saw that they had a lot of turkeys. But I wasn't totally convinced and I tried to choose one because they said it was fresh and they didn't put it in the refrigerator. Suddenly I started to not feel very good. I had walked a long way trying to find a turkey that I didn't have to thaw. I came home tired, but decided to cook it that night because I didn't want to feel tired the next day. To this day I don't know what happened, but when I went to carve the turkey early in the morning I saw that it had a skin that was cracking as well as all the meat. I realized that I was not going to be able to cut it because it was falling apart and I went to the market to buy another one. There was only one that wasn't frozen and I bought it. In the rush I forgot that the stuffing I had was thrown away with the other turkey I bought. A lot of things went wrong and I had to work all morning to be ready when the guests arrived. I was more looking forward to going to bed than having visitors. But I don't know what I did. No one said anything to me, to top it off one of my friends praised me so much on how well I cooked that I felt bad. Nobody said anything. Only my sister said I was a bad housewife. And I don't know if she was also referring to the fiasco that turned out to be my dinner. Even though I wanted to, I found it hard to stay awake. Because I was so tired, I was glad that I had finished dinner while still being a fiasco.

The week of Christmas was not a pleasant one for many. There was again talk of a new virus. I don't remember when I heard that you couldn't travel without getting tested within 24 hours to travel abroad. And many started to tell me that I had better postpone my trip. But I didn't want to listen to anyone and decided to travel. I could not take the test before the stipulated time. When it was time to travel, the test had not arrived and I started to go crazy. In the end, the person who was helping me told me to go to the airport. I think he told me I could take the test at Kennedy Airport. But when I got to where I was told they were doing it, I wanted to leave my bags and the airport was empty. Someone from the airlines told me that to take the test I had to leave the airport and I would find a place to take the test. When I was in line waiting, someone came out and told us that they were charging $200. But someone added that we still could not travel until the next day because the result took I don't know how long and we were very close to the time the plane was due to leave. Others appeared who had heard that the vaccine worked, but when we arrived they told us the same as the first time, that we could not travel until we had the test result. I went back into the airport and when I found where to check my bag, I was told that my plane had already left. The airport was deserted and my plane was already in the air. I started to walk around not knowing how to get out of the airport when I saw many people offering to carry passengers. But none of them were doing long trips. Suddenly, someone told me that he could take me to where there was a small bus going to Philadelphia, picking up passengers in certain places. One person offered to take me to the place where it was leaving. It was cold and I was tired and hungry and we had to wait in a corner. The boy was very kind and accompanied me until the small bus arrived. We arrived in Philadelphia in the rain and, to make matters worse, a car hit us as we were arriving at my home. Fortunately my sister Herminia was waiting for me and a young woman lent me the phone to call her, because I had the key to the house, it was snowing and I thought it would be a bother to open the suitcase.

I arrived at my condo tired and starving. Thanks to Herminia I was able to eat something hot and she left because it was still snowing and we were afraid that she would also have an accident. Alone I felt so sad that I didn't know what to do and I fell fast asleep after taking two sleeping pills.

The next day, I woke up dizzy, but I threw a tantrum and angrily emptied my suitcase. Many people told me that maybe it was for my own good that I didn't go. I spent the day trying to forget, but in the afternoon the person who had helped me so much called me. He told me to go again for the test and that he was sure it would go well, that he would receive it early in the morning and that I would be ready. The night came and still no news about the test. I decided to empty my suitcases because it was almost midnight and I didn't want to be completely disappointed. Anyway, I thought, I didn't keep everything. The only thing I hid was the Argentinean money I had and it was quite a lot because two years ago when I went to Argentina I did not spend so much because I had so many problems to travel. When I saw that they did not call me to tell me that I had the result, I took two sleeping pills again.

Again my friend called me. But this time he told me to turn on the copier because he would send me the proof. I asked him to wait to make the copy for fear that something was wrong and my printer would not work. Everything went fine, and with the test in my hands

I put it in my wallet. But again I felt that I had forgotten something. I slept nervously because I had to talk to the agency to change my ticket. In the end I left the next day thinking that everything was fine. The trip was incredible. There were several unoccupied seats. I thought that many had had problems and the silence was total. I slept well, but I imagine that so many problems were making me sick. I did everything like I was on clouds and what surprised me the most was how easy it was for me to fall asleep. I would wake up dizzy. Thank God I made the plane transfer from Ezeiza to Bariloche without any problems.

I had a hard time recognizing my brother at the airport and I almost had a problem because when I saw my suitcase and approached to take it a man stepped forward and took it out of the lane. I told him it was my bag and he told me it was his because he always put yellow tape on it to recognize it. Thank God my suitcase has a pocket where I have my name card.

We arrived safely at my sister Juana's house, but I guess I didn't look too good because she told me she was going to make me some tea and to go to bed early. I, while she went to the kitchen to make me tea, lay down on a couch. It didn't look anything like mine, but I thought I hadn't traveled and was on the couch at home. I said to Juana, "When did you get here?" because I thought I was at my house. Juana got quite a laugh out of it because she says I looked really shocked and didn't understand why I thought she was at my house. We laughed when I finally told her that I was probably very tired.

But that was not all. For some days I would forget everything. And I would go back to thinking I was at home. Well, the family thought it was very funny. But it worried me. Thank God that seemed to have happened to me before. Gradually I got back to normal. But I keep thinking that it took me a while to find out that this can happen when you find yourself in trouble like what was happening to me because of the pandemic. I had come to Bariloche with something on my mind and I thought I would not return to the United States until I knew what happened to the books I had left two years before.

That had me worried and I couldn't wait to feel well enough to call the printer where I had left some of the books I had brought the last time I was in Bariloche and others I had mailed. I knew that until I saw the owner of the printer I would not be at peace. This time I had made more progress in my idea of publishing my book in my hometown and I also had a feeling that this time I would manage to see my books in all the bookstores in my hometown.

CHAPTER

4

And the day came when I managed to make an appointment with the owner of the printing company. I went to see him. I expected him to tell me that he had made progress and had already left some books on consignment. But, of course, I did not remember that I had not yet signed a contract and I began to think that maybe I had come and there was not enough time to get everything ready. I knew that it was not going to be so easy and to make matters worse, when I wanted to pay him for the books I had left and others I had brought, when I looked in my wallet for the money I had set aside to pay him I found that the envelope I had prepared to pay the owner of the printing house had been left the night I thought I should listen to all those who told me that maybe if I had so many problems to travel to Argentina it was a sign that it was not in my destiny to do so, but I was not willing to back out. I was even more angry when someone told me that it was a sign that I was not going to do well. I didn't answer because I'm not superstitious. But I thought it was ridiculous to be told that. Superstitious or not, I preferred to think that whenever I wanted to do something I had a hard time achieving it and if I succeeded, even if only half-heartedly, in some attempts I made to put my books on sale, I think I was a coward for not daring to fight. If I succeeded in other things in my life, it was because I did not give up until I got what I wanted. Suddenly I told myself that this time I will not lose. And I will not stop fighting until I reach my goal and see my books once again in the windows of the bookstores in Bariloche. And why not, in other countries.

I went back to my sister's house so depressed that I wanted to cry. But I swallowed my pride and thought I should calm down and let the person who was helping me act as he should. I thought about telling her to send me the money I was missing, but I quickly thought that would be a problem. I decided to go slowly. Many times I had failed to do something I wanted to do because I was not patient and didn't do things right. I didn't even insist on telling the man at the printer's that I would have liked to see the books in the bookstores before returning to the States. I didn't say anything because we went to drop off the books and had to walk a long way. I wanted to do things right and I didn't want to miss seeing which bookstore had agreed to leave my books on consignment which I think is the best way to put them in the windows.

In Bariloche, tourism had opened up, but it was only for Argentines. At first it seemed to me that the use of the mask was more respected than in the United States, but I soon saw that some of my relatives did not. I did not want to judge. In the center of town many respected the rules of covering their faces and disinfecting their hands. That got me out sometimes to visit some of my family members, even those who had had the virus, but it had not been fatal to anyone I knew. Still, I didn't feel safe and didn't feel like going out. I had left the money I had left over two years before. It wasn't much, but I tried not to say anything. It took me a long time to talk about what it took to get to Bariloche and I was even afraid that my family would find out how bad I felt. Again, I tried not to say anything. I was afraid that in the end I would have to ask them to lend me money and in doing so I would be forced to tell them everything bad that happened to me and how hard it was for me to make it without asking for a loan.

The days continued to pass and the date to return was approaching. I had heard nothing more about the printing company. When suddenly they called me and asked me if I had opened a bank account and I said no. The truth is that I had tried to do so and had gone to a bank where I was told how difficult it would be at that time to open a bank account. The truth is that I had tried to do so and had gone to a bank where I was told how difficult it would be at that time to open an account in my name. I had already tried to go into a bank to ask, but they told me I would have to make an appointment. I saw the line of people waiting to be served and I got scared. I remembered everything I went through trying to travel. The pain from standing too long due to my arthritis tortured me more than ever.

Suddenly I remembered again that it had been days since I had spoken to the man at the printer's and I hadn't heard from him. I didn't understand why he hadn't called me to see how things were going. Again I began to think that this would be another one of those times I had paid to put a book in the bookstores and I felt the same sadness I experienced then, when I thought I was never going to share my books with anyone. I began to think that I should stop dreaming and enjoy the money I had by fulfilling other desires. But which one? I would choose whenever I thought I was capable of succeeding in something, but very quickly I would abandon my dream. At one time it was to dance Argentine folklore. However, when I had a chance to do it, I saw that I was not even graceful enough to dance. Everything remained an illusion. I also tried to think and sometimes I remembered that I had been highly praised at school because I was good at drawing. But I could never get very far, it always got in the way of me not being able to live with my parents so that I could have finished one of the many careers I started and had to leave because I didn't live in a city or have a home where I could take refuge in case I lost a job.

And so 84 years passed for me. Many praised me for having wrinkle-free skin for the age I was. I would look in the mirror and look younger than I was. But that vanity didn't last long for me. One day I was looking in the mirror and I saw that I had some spots on my neck. Then they appeared on my face. I went to a dermatologist and he told me that sometimes that happened, blamed it on my age and prescribed a rather expensive cream. When I finished using it, I realized that it had no effect. My face was getting worse and worse and so was my neck. The medicine only left my skin more wrinkled than it was and even having tried all the skin blemish creams I am beginning to believe that they will never say to me, "What beautiful skin you have for the age you are." Nothing had had any effect and my skin was much worse. But I remember that I complained to the doctor again and he prescribed another cream that didn't work either. The spots, which at first were red, turned black and my complexion, which I had been praised so many times, was almost blackish brown and wrinkled. I never heard anything about whether it had anything to do with the pandemic. I started looking at everyone in the market because that was the only place I had visited in over two years. Some people, usually blondes, were so red in the face, I wondered if it was because they had been out in the sun a lot or it had to do with the viruses they advertised for two years. And it wasn't a sunburn. Anyway, the loneliness in which I shut myself up made me think I was going crazy. And I started to imagine things.

Going back to my failed attempt to do something with my books, I remember feeling so bad, but trying to make my family believe that I was having a good time. To disguise it, I would tell them that I didn't feel like going out much because the arthritis I had wouldn't let me walk. That was true. But it was the idea that they would find out that I had almost no money and I was afraid that they would invite me out and then I wouldn't be able to find a way out of what was happening to me. A few times someone in the family invited me to visit a place I really wanted to see and we went to see I don't know how many lakes. All beautiful. I thought God had rewarded us Barilochenses with such beautiful landscapes, which sometimes makes me wonder why I left my city at such a young age. I can't find an answer that tells me and I think that maybe at my young age I didn't know what I had. I only know that since I was a child I imagined myself going far away.

Regarding the situation in which I found myself, I can say that I cannot find an answer to the many questions that come to my mind when I think of what I went through during those days. There was one day, when I was almost ready to go back to Philadelphia, when I decided to call the printer and tell the person who had my books to forget everything and that I had decided to go back. But just as I made that crazy decision, the owner of the printer called me to tell me that they had the books and everything ready for me to go with him the next day to drop off some books at bookstores. I hadn't slept well and my leg was hurting so bad, but I wasn't going to do something to ruin everything like I had done so many times before. I got in the car not caring if I was in pain or not. It was a few hours of getting in the car and getting out in some car parking lot, sometimes climbing stairs and walking when we couldn't park near the bookstore where we would drop off some books and do the book presentation. Thank God, everyone seemed to know the man in the print shop and I just smiled and let him talk. I didn't feel like I have when I have gone to a book fair in the United States and had to do the presentation, but it was different there. I had been given a class on what to say, here it was different, I was just going to be introduced to the owners of the bookstore. It seems to me that the owner of the printing house had already left a book for them to read. Thank God that made me feel better. I was so dejected that I was glad I didn't have the responsibility of doing it all myself. I even took a nap when I got back to my sister's house where I was staying. I felt like a huge weight had been lifted off my shoulders.

Some of my family members are not big talkers. And since no one seemed to care much about what I did, I didn't give them much information. But I do tell my two younger sisters and other family members, especially when they ask me questions where I see that there is an interest in what I do or don't do. And from Toya, one of my sisters, I found out that the books were out and they made a presentation of them. Well at least I have taken a step forward. I did this years ago when I wrote "La sombra del Barón", a book based on my childhood. What happened was that I took that book with the idea of making some copies. When I worked in Buenos Aires, I was between 18 and 26 years old, I studied English with a person who helped me a lot. She always told me: "Let me help you because I love you as if I were your mother. Whatever problem you have let me help you." In the first years of my stay in the United States we corresponded, but suddenly I didn't see her anymore. Then we started to communicate by mail and when I went to visit her I told her that I had published some books and she suggested that I send her some to read. Then she advised me to translate them. I said yes, but I told her about "La sombra del barón", I told her that I was only sending it to her to read because it was a book from my childhood and I knew that my family would not like it because in it I wrote about my childhood and there were things that nobody would like. I stressed to him again that he should only publish the other book, which I don't remember the name of. I did not go to Argentina for more than two years and, when I returned, my older brother told me that he saw the book in a bookstore and since he had a granddaughter named Laura he thought she had written it. Many years later I was encouraged to ask what had happened to the book. One of my sisters told me, when I asked her a long time ago, what had happened, but I really don't know until now. My brother and other people told me that they had seen it. But I couldn't know anything else. I do know that some people thought it was very bad that I had written a book according to them so strong. But there is also someone who read it and thought he didn't see anything so terrible to make such a big deal about it. That's all I know from my experience as a writer in my town. I don't want to think anything with what would happen if something comes along again that some people don't like, but I understand.

In life there are things that happen to many people and sometimes you may think that you are listening to something that you know is not new because something similar has happened to you so far away. But it usually happens. It has happened to me to be in a group of people and hear that what someone is saying, who I don't even know, has happened to someone I know. Well, I already have experience with readers getting angry, as a friend told me when I wrote my first book in Philadelphia. I think she got angry because she thought I was describing the main character in the novel as she was. Either by chance I had introduced her as she was or maybe something similar to what happened to my character had happened to her.

I remember that friend introduced me to a man who gave English classes to people who had just arrived from other countries. I was one of his favorite students because he knew Spanish. First he gave me a book and told me that I would find a topic to use. He would give me the words and I would make sentences with them. Then I saw that the book was the same one my last English teacher used and I pointed it out to him. I wanted to write, look up words in the dictionary. Then I started to imagine everything in my own way. I invented a newcomer from Argentina as he wanted and added other people. Without realizing it, I started to invent like when I was in school. He told me to write about newcomers. I started writing about my friend who was recently in Philadelphia. I imagined what the trip had been like and suddenly I brought it to life and started, like I did in school and my teacher would ask me if I was making up what I was writing. Yes, that was what I liked to do. It was comfortable for me too, I lived on Spruce Street and I started my class, I saw that I was just repeating what I had learned with other teachers and I pointed it out to him. He asked me why I didn't write something about my life. And so I started to free write. He also told me to draw ideas from what I was living, I thought I would write not about people but about what I saw in the news but I told the professor that, in order not to confuse me, I was going to put names of people I knew. I never thought that what I had invented could have happened to the people I thought were a figment of my imagination. We were a group of women doing the same jobs. Our lives were somewhat similar in many ways. Most of us were just starting to learn English. Some of us were going to the same place for classes. On Sundays we would get together. Whenever any of us met a new person I was sure to bring them to the apartment we rented to get together on Sundays.

Nowhere in my book is anything mentioned that is rude or said with bad intentions. But the professor told me he had written a novel and helped me translate it into English. The characters have nothing to do with the two friends, but it was one of them who said I was doing business by making up and telling private things about their lives. Only one of them accused me, told me that she cursed me and that she was going to see to it that I never wrote again. I thought it was the most ridiculous thing that could happen to me. I wrote the book in Spanish and the professor translated it for me because I found an ad, I think it was in one of the Philadelphia newspapers, that said they could publish ten books for two hundred dollars and that was my first step as a writer. I gave some of them away to several friends and one of them who knew English read it to all the friends who would listen. But one of them repeated that I was trying to make money by badmouthing them. I told them all that I hadn't taken them into account at all when I wrote the book and that I didn't think I was going to make much by selling 20 books. When I told the professor what had happened to me he told me not to make trouble.

I had a hard time with my first book, but even though I was 26 years old, I thought I would have time to be able to say I was a writer. My ambitions were not fulfilled perhaps because nothing was easy for me. Everything had cost me in life and, as a child, I considered myself to be an unlucky person. I started going to school at the age of 8. It was because I begged my mother a lot to talk to my maternal grandmother to allow me to live in her house. But she said she had no place for me because she had Perico, my half-brother, and Silvia, my older sister, at home to go to school. There was no room for anyone else. I spent days walking around sad. Silvia, my sister, who is a year older than me, would go back to her grandmother and go to second grade. But I was lucky that my older brother, who also lived at grandma's house, was called up for military service because he was twenty years old. So I started studying. I would have been one of the oldest in my grade, they had a law that said everyone had to go to school until they were fourteen.

I had already learned to write a little at home. We used to have some of dad's friends visiting us for a few days. They always saw me drawing, because I liked to do it, and my mother bought me a notebook and pencils every time I went to Bariloche. I loved animals and I liked to draw them. But I was always a trouble maker. Once I wanted to draw a dog that was in a book and I had the idea of taking the measurements of the drawing because I wanted to do it as I saw it. I don't think the drawing came out that well. But when the teacher came to correct it, she told me that the drawing I had done was a perfect copy. A classmate told her that I had traced it. Tracing was called making a copy of the original in those days. The teacher told the boy that I had made a copy, but he thought the teacher was lying to make me look good. I never understood why my classmate imposed himself to make me look bad. That left a bitter taste in my mouth. The boy, I don't remember his name, stopped being my friend. It was the first time I was accused of lying. It hurt me a lot.

CHAPTER 5

Lately I've been having a hard time going back to my current life. I am starting to think that lately I am living remembering my past and I think that is what makes me think that I am an old person. It is normal that sometimes when I am doing something, my mind plays a trick on me, I forget what I was doing and I feel a little disoriented. But that happens more when I'm talking and suddenly I don't know what I was talking about. I find that in front of the computer I concentrate more on what I am experiencing and I can remember where my mind stopped and pick up a conversation. Sometimes someone notices and they ignore what is happening to me and say, maybe to comfort me: "That happens to me too". And I go back and remember where I left off in what I was talking about and continue to talk about what I was talking about. But, in my last visit to my family in Argentina, we realized that we were all in the same problem because we were only a year and months apart from each other when we were born. So there is not a big difference in age between one and the other of us.

On my last visit I was not so lonely. When we got together we would laugh at each other. And if we were reminiscing about something that had happened when we were together, each of us would add something to the narrative that had been left out. I was at my sister's house, the family gave me a hand, and I thought surely everything would be easier. As well as some friends in the United States who helped me to travel to Argentina. This time I went to my sister Juana's house and her nephews helped me from the moment I arrived at the house. One of them took me in his car to take the COVID test to return to the United States. It was easier because I had made an appointment and they just gave me the test I needed to travel and I went back home with it. After lunch they took me to the Bariloche airport and asked me for a wheelchair. I felt good with the help and I rested knowing that they, besides asking me for a wheelchair, were with me until I did all the paperwork. Already at the airport in Buenos Aires they were waiting for me with the chair that was going to take me to the places where I had to leave to take the flight to the United States. There I was also taken from one place to another and it took a while because I was told that the suitcase was going straight to Kennedy airport. But there was one person who wanted to be sure that with hers there would be no problem because she thought that she should have been told that she would only see the suitcase when she arrived in the United States. She was adamant and ordered them to be brought to her because she would ship them. She kept repeating that the suitcases should have been with her all the time until she sent them. In the end there were two of us who had to go to where they would confirm that Aerolineas Argentinas would see to it that they arrived at Kennedy Airport. I was already beginning to think the worst, when we got to where they told us that they would ask if we had to take the suitcase with us or not. It seemed to me that we were too late and that we might miss the plane. But they took us to a place where the person who had made so much trouble was able to talk to us on the phone and we finally made it to the place where the plane was leaving.

    I understood that we were in pandemic time, the only thing that mattered to me was that I didn't get infected. But I still had to get to Philadelphia and face what awaited me. Again I found myself thinking that I had no idea how I would get home. I looked to see if there was anyone with a sign offering a means of locomotion. But

I didn't see one that was a cab. The only thing I saw was a man who seemed to be waiting for someone and suddenly I saw that it was not a cab, but someone flagged him down and told him to wait. He went in where we came out and came back helping a passenger with his bags. I asked him if he knew how to find a cab. Luckily he told me that the car that had just left belonged to a friend. He asked me if I wanted him to call him because the passengers he was carrying were not going very far. I sat and waited outside the airport.

I finally made it home. I felt tired and even admired myself for having endured so much. I felt dizzy but that was not the end of my problems. I didn't have enough money to pay for the cab and thank God I found money in a wallet I had in a coat I always used to wear when I went shopping. I was able to get to my condo. The next day, I woke up early, still feeling groggy. I had breakfast and looked for the mail which was a lot. The first thing that brought me back to reality was when I saw a notice on the computer telling me to try to pay my taxes as soon as possible. I had to do that every time I came back from Argentina. The next day I got into my car which made me feel that I was far away from my payments. But since everything was the same as the previous year it didn't take me long to bring my accounts up to date. Slowly I started to get back to my routine. But for the first time in my life I felt like I was helpless and I cried. Because there are two things I can never do, they are cry or feel defeated. I always put a good face on bad weather. But since COVID 19 started, more than two years ago, I feel so lonely and sad that I really want to cry. I was never a crier. But when I analyze my life I see that it has never been easy. I have to do something because I can't keep disappearing from the contagion that seems to have no end. Just when I decided to drop the mask they announce that another virus is coming. The idea of being afraid of being infected again makes me feel bad. I, who have always been one to not sit still, find it difficult to have to avoid being around many people. Although a little desolation I was dreading because since I came to the United States I met a lot of people. I always had a group of friends to invite over for lunch, go see a show, or get together for a picnic in a park when I lived in Philadelphia.

While I lived with my husband in Ocean City I only made a few meetings. But I led a life where it was easy to make friends. Since my husband passed away I have led a rather lonely life. I had a hard time getting used to his absence. I don't think I would ever have married if I hadn't met Michael, he had what I expected for a marriage. There was a companionship and understanding between us that made us always happy. Also, we were two people who, although we didn't even look alike physically, were alike in our way of thinking. There was a mutual understanding between us. From him I learned to look into religion because I did not have an education or knowledge that made me understand what it meant to be Catholic. In church I was always bored when I didn't know or understand what it was like to participate in a mass. But I managed to learn the prayers, I learned to sing the songs and little by little I saw that for me it was a duty. I was happy to do it, especially when I went with my husband. We enjoyed learning the songs and going to church every Sunday and feast day made me feel good. We both came back from church happy that we had fulfilled our Christian duty. We didn't work that day and usually went to a restaurant or cooked together.

When we both found out that I didn't like to work in the garden we made an arrangement that he would take care of the yard work, fix the house when necessary, take me to the market and we would do the shopping between the two of us. My life in Ocean City was very pleasant until Michael, who had been in the hospital many times since I met him, began to feel sick more and more. After two years of having a nurse in the house, I was told that I could no longer care for him and had to admit him. I was beginning to believe that he would recover and come home, but that was not to be and I did not know what to do when I was told there was nothing more I could do. I knew there was nothing I could do and I had to let him go.

Why did I remember it all day today? I don't know. Maybe because I don't feel very well or maybe something has made me think of him.

But something always leads me to not being able to accept that he's gone. It must be because I'm lonely and it makes me angry. Sometimes it's as if I think I wasn't as good and patient with him as he was with me. But I know it couldn't have been any other way. For me having to hospitalize him more than once started to be very sad and I suffered mentally. He fought until he was gone and nothing lets me forget him. But now the memory of him is less and less painful for me. I try to believe that God has him in a place where everything is less complicated as it is in this world we live in. And it is better to think that he is better off than me at this moment because I feel very sad. I think I'm a masochist because I don't mind suffering. But I know that I am like that. I don't think like some people who don't want to get vaccinated because they think, if the virus is going to attack them, it's going to attack them, period. But some have learned the lesson, they have done it when they got infected or lost a loved one. I have many in my family who survived having been infected. I will try to have a quiet day.

Anyway, a few days ago I went back to the Adult Center where I work out. I was happy to see that some people I hadn't seen for two years were doing well. Many were noticeable that, like me, they had not dyed their hair and were white with gray. Others had aged a bit. Few welcomed me and were glad to see me. I would have liked to ask how they lived those years. Also, it seemed to me that some had not done very well and it would have been interesting to ask them if they had a good time or had changed a lot. I expected them to welcome me and very few did. None made a comment about what it was like for them to endure more than two years of pandemic. None said whether they had been vaccinated or not. It was as if the pandemic had happened long ago and no one even wanted to remember it. For a moment I thought the pandemic was something that happened a long time ago and everyone had forgotten about it. I found myself as if something I imagined was happening to me, something that was like a movie that had a life while it was on the screen and that everyone forgot about as soon as they left the theater. But in my mind it will surely remain for a while longer.

We'll see how long it takes me to get back to my life of the last few years. I have changed a lot. But no one seemed to notice that I have white hair. I didn't want to dye it because I had promised to take the best care of myself and I was afraid to go to a salon for fear of catching it. No one made any comments. It seemed to me that many of the attendees were missing. There were very few of us wearing a mask. After inquiring, I saw that only a few of us had been infected. I began to think that perhaps by going back to the places I used to frequent I would begin to feel less desolate. Although I knew well that nothing was going to repeat itself and be like before. But I could have been satisfied if I could rescue a little of what I was and what I went through in the past. Sometimes I think that, when the few remaining friends get together, we should stop complaining about the many aches and pains that old age brings and start living the years we have left, enjoying what we can do and what we have left to live. Well, why keep complaining, why not talk about good things? I'm thinking of taking some drawing classes because I want to make some pictures with the photos I have of the last house where my parents lived. I don't know if I'll make it. But I'm going to try. I have to find a way to keep busy and what better than doing something that I would like to enjoy again… so many things I did in the past, find new friends and get closer to the few I have left.

I don't know why I watch television if all they show is misery. Human beings are becoming less and less human. The media do not help. What they show the most are the crimes that are committed every day, instead of talking about the scientific advances that are helping the human being to live a better life. Science has advanced in medicines and in curing many diseases, this makes human beings live longer. But we don't hear that much in the media. Nobody seems to want to educate the human being about the progress in science that helps us in so many things. On the front page we see how many people die at the hands of some madman who pulls the trigger without mercy. They don't care about the age of the person they killed, the important thing is to take the life of whoever gets in the way. It seems that for some humans it is more important to satisfy their desire to kill. It no longer matters if there are cameras that record everything. The criminal instinct of thinking that the one who has a weapon is more powerful and they know how to manage to satisfy their instinct, I do not say animal because most animals only kill to eat. How to understand that there can be such cruel beings?

Yesterday I was supposed to go to art class. But I thought I was going to waste my time because I didn't buy what I need to get started. I get mad at myself for making such a big deal out of everything. Here I am in front of my computer, which sometimes makes me want to throw it away, because every day I have problems with it and it's driving me crazy. I never know why they don't leave me alone. I don't know who, but they fill my computer with ads. I think they used to be called viruses. I never understood how they could. According to the notices I read, every time I sat down to write they were made by people who know how to lie and make innocent people fall who can't think that someone is trying to make them fall into their trap. For example, it seems that many people know that I have published some books. I even seem to hear the same warning over and over again. Because they sometimes tell me that they can help me publish more and that they are offering to take me to fame for less money than I am paying. They name the book I just wrote and promise me to take it to book fairs to exhibit it and make me known. I fell into that trap several times and exhibited the books at the fair because they told me I could sell them there. But they only gave me an hour where the time I spent talking about the content of my book was wasted. They also made me buy a number of books and I didn't even sell enough to replace the money I spent renting an exhibition space. It is very easy to fall into these traps. One learns and falls into the same thing again. Until one day you say enough is enough. In some corner of the house there are books taking up space when they could be in a bookstore where one could donate them. Because after having read so many books, one never stops thinking that there is something for everyone who loves reading. And so you keep thinking that you really wrote a good book, but you end up keeping it in case someday you can really find someone who really thinks that time you might be lucky enough to make a way for yourself. If you think about it, how do you know if it wasn't true when they told you they had a good market for your book and you missed a good opportunity to make yourself known and achieve your desire for your book to be read, even if only by someone.

CHAPTER

6

Today is a very hot day. I am thankful that I have nothing to do and I will take the opportunity to add something I was remembering. Today it came to my mind when to go to school I had to live with a relative. This time I remember I was with my maternal grandmother. I don't remember how old I was, but I do remember that sometimes I felt like going out with some friends. I was invited, however, I had been taught not to accept going out unless it was with a relative or someone that my grandmother knew. While I was with my mother's mother I tried, but they told me the same thing. They couldn't let me go out because they didn't know what kind of people were inviting me and they thought it was strange that a schoolmate could have the freedom to invite me to her house. Because both my grandmother and my aunt, who lived with her, didn't feel reassured that we were going to an unfamiliar house. But when my best friend invited me for the second time, I lied to grandma saying that the teacher suggested I go give a classmate a hand. On one occasion, the teacher who knew my aunt asked her permission to let me go. But this time it was not the same person and my grandmother thought it was strange that the teacher had not called her. The truth is that I had such a good time. The mother spoke to her in English which was the language she knew best. While she was talking to me she would ask my friend to translate what we were talking about.

I was always curious to know what life was like in Europe, the continent from which many families immigrated to Argentina after World War II. From that day on I started to ask many of my classmates and I noticed that especially the boys did not like to answer me. Those who were older did not like it so much. I never understood why so many left their countries and it was my father who told me it was because of the wars. When I asked him why there were wars, he told me: "those gringos are always fighting among themselves". And from then on I settled for thinking that it was like what happened when my brothers and I fought with each other, until mom or dad intervened we wouldn't stop arguing.

I would have asked my friend questions because I still didn't understand why there were wars. At that time, people came to my city from all over Europe. There were many who came after the Second World War. Since I liked to build castles in the air, I began to wonder what it would be like if my parents had come from other countries and I could, like my friend, speak two languages. My paternal grandfather was Spanish Basque and my grandmother was Peruvian. On my mother's side she was Chilean. My friend's mother asked her to tell me to come back again. But my grandmother suspected that I had lied and the second time my friend invited me she told me that I had no reason to go to strangers' houses.

That vacation, when I returned home, I discovered that the room was lined with magazines showing beautiful places. But since I didn't understand the language, I thought they were landscapes of Germany. I lived dreaming that one day I would travel to other countries and speak another language. Not like the owners of the ranch where my father worked, who were German, but never bothered to learn Spanish because they always had an interpreter to translate for them. I would hear them speak when they came to tell my father something and I would try hard to understand them. We always thought they were the owners of the estancia. But in time we found out that they were only the ones in charge of one of the ranches. Years later I found out more, when a book about the Nazis in Bariloche revealed the history of the place.

In the year I was in school many Europeans came and, since I wrote well, the teacher sat them at my table so that I could help them speak and write Spanish. There were few of us who had that privilege. I was happy to help, but other students didn't like having to do it. Too bad it didn't occur to me to exchange words. Perhaps, if I had learned English or another language when I was a child, I would not have as much trouble pronouncing English well as I do now. I see that I spent my life making castles in the air and now that I start to think that I am a few years old I see that I did not understand that I missed several opportunities to have taken advantage of what life gave me.

At this moment a gaucho poem comes to mind that says: "Some are born with the star and others are born starry." I don't think I was born with the star because I haven't achieved much in this life. But fatality and having had to live away from home in order to go to school meant that I had many ups and downs in my life. Some people think I was lucky to have lived my childhood knowing and learning to get used to living in different homes with different people, each one trying to impose their way of life on me. Not seeing my parents only for the vacations, which at that time were in winter, made me live always waiting for the day when we would return home. But the snow, which seemed to me to be stronger, made me stay more indoors. Still, spending it at home and with the family I didn't see for most of the year was a blessing. At home everything was bliss, my mother did not do like other mothers I knew because she never forced us to take care of our siblings. I would visit some families and I would always see the older sister taking care of the younger ones. I had the impression that they never played. They were not educated either until Perón forced all the ranchers to help by putting up rural schools in the countryside and in small towns and estancias. In this way he made it possible for some of the children of those who worked on the ranches to learn at least to read and write.

I think that's why I'm glad I didn't have children. Because there are many friends who tell me that they never imagined how difficult it is to be a mother. But surely there are many women who have been happy and feel proud of having lived being good mothers and having managed to lead a happy life. I also say this for the men who have been able to be good fathers and have brought children into the world that make them proud. Sorry if I said something I shouldn't have. But now that we are in pandemic time and I am living a life that is too quiet, I am reminded of things from my past that I no longer remembered. My mind seems to be living more in the past than in the present and I seem to remember so many things, fragments of good times and bad.

Today was a day when I felt happy. I went to the Adult Center where I do gymnastics and I also take an art class. I also went to a store. I was proud of myself because I had made a resolution not to go unless I had a need and I did because in over two years I have only gone to the market. A few times I have gone to the park to spend a few hours. I think many will think I'm exaggerating. But since hardly anyone wears the mask anymore, I don't feel safe without the protection. When I go to exercise there are very few of us who protect ourselves, most people don't wear the mask. But, anyway, I think I'm going to start going back to my old life because with four vaccinations I can stop worrying so much. The president is also infected. I better stop being so pessimistic and resolve to start living a more normal life. I don't mind wearing the mask or taking care of myself as much as possible. But if I lock myself up I don't think I'm going to accomplish much. I accept one more vaccine and keep taking care of myself.

I have been trying to get back to my old life and I keep thinking that the world of friends I had is no more. Most of them were from Argentina. In the first years of living in the United States I had a hard time finding someone to make friends with. At first it was because of the language. I had studied English several times, but I had trouble pronouncing it. It wasn't until I met my husband that I could say that I started to make myself understood. And I was able to really have American friends. I never had problems writing, so when I took some classes I was able to make progress especially writing and reading, which was what I liked to do most. Sometimes I also think that one of the problems I have is that it's enough for me to do something wrong and I fall apart. Being so demanding with myself is what never made me achieve several goals that I set out to achieve and didn't achieve them.

I keep trying to take my life to a higher degree. But I think it's too late to try to do something I like, like painting landscape paintings. This time I won't run a race against time. I will go about trying to get my desires nice and slow. Because I am no longer in a position to say that I have a life ahead of me. During the last few years, even though I have been very quiet because of the pandemic, time has flown by and I am starting to think differently. I only ask God to help me, that the arthritis pain I have I can bear. But I must remember that I have fought a lot against a disease that has many ways of attacking. A year ago I had pain in my back and legs. I managed to make those pains go away. But the one I can't seem to fight is the one in my left leg. I will campaign to convert it because I still have things left to do in this world. I do not intend to give up without managing to write what may be my last biography. I cannot let myself be defeated by a pain that surely wants to get in the way of the projects I have for my future.

Sometimes I think about my husband...what it would be like if he were around. I remember him again... what he was like when I first met him. It was like everything in my life was like before. Because when I go to Bariloche and I'm with my family and we start reminiscing about our past, it seems that over the years we all remember something different and there's no shortage of people who raise their voices and get quiet and we stay quiet or we don't want to give in. We remain silent or there is someone who leaves us without comment. Those of us who were right raise our heads with an air of triumph. But there have been moments when we are left with the pain of recognizing that we have lost. And we keep silent for a long time and there is someone who to break the silence talks about something else and everything makes us remember, as my mother or my father always said, there should be no quarrels between siblings. That usually happens when we get together to eat. Sometimes the one who cooked the meat arrives, because for Argentines there is no meeting if there is no barbecue and a good wine, and we all go to the table and finish the meeting as good brothers.

I think that in Argentina and in many countries the only time men were seen helping to cook was when the family got together and they made the asado. In my house, when relatives who lived in town, as we called Bariloche, came to my house, we would see dad in front of the stove with an air of feeling superior because he thought that as the owner of the house it was his duty to show how to make a good asado. Mom was in charge of the empanadas, which are different all over the country. It was not customary for many people to praise the cook because it was quite normal that "the boss", as mother was called that day, did not need to be told that everything was tasty. When we didn't have visitors we all cooked, but when relatives came, the children would gather on one side and the older ones on the other. Then we would reminisce about the old years of our youth and give everything a good end to a Sunday with the family.

I won't stop thinking about the past, even though it doesn't always bring back good memories. It also makes me prone to relive more the good happy times of my childhood, because I liked to draw and read. I think I learned that pleasure from my mother who, although she had not gone to school for a long time had the lower first book saved. My father also had books of Creole verses and liked to recite poetry and songs alluding to country life. In the city I felt oppressed. I didn't have the freedom I had in the countryside. To be able to run without being told to be careful not to break your shoes. Or to walk slowly because my grandmothers and aunts were afraid that we would fall. I remember how patient my mother was with us. Coming home on vacations was a blessing. But Dad, who was a bit of a macho man, didn't like us riding horses. That privilege in that part of my life was with my brother José, who was born after four women. Dad bought him a guitar when he was very young. For me it was terrible that when relatives who lived in Bariloche or others from the city of Buenos Aires came to visit us and for national holidays like May 25th, which is the day of freedom, my father and my brother would show off. I ignored them while I entertained myself playing with my cousins. But Christmas was for everyone.

I don't remember how old I was when Evita Perón sent toys and cider to all the workers and farm workers. Then even the children drank cider, a sweet drink, and there was no shortage of sweet bread. But since they were all rather big families and there were many children, a little cider wouldn't be bad for them.

In the long run I live with the thought that, compared to the life of some of my classmates, we didn't have such a bad time. The teachers did their best to make us learn. As I said before, there were many children who arrived after the war and some of them did not know a word of Spanish. It seemed to be my destiny, because when I arrived in the United States I had a hard time understanding how to pronounce English. Although in Buenos Aires, when I worked before coming to the United States, I went for two years to study the language in a very good academy. I had a teacher who always told me, "Laura, pronounce well, don't speak like those Americans who pronounce so badly." That hurt me a little because I was never one to speak badly of anyone, nor to criticize. We don't speak Spanish the way it is spoken in Spain. But who cares, we all try to do our best. For example, I can't pronounce English like Americans do either. But I try. No human being is perfect. The important thing is to try to do everything we can to the best of our ability. Thank God I don't need to be a language scholar. I wish I could have found a way to speak it, but as long as I can write I console myself and keep trying to speak as best I can.

It has been a long time ago, but I don't know why I always remember the past more clearly than the present time in which I am living. It is August and in a few days I will be 84 years old. Today I took the time to go back and feel so empty, as if in this life time has stopped. Suddenly I think I should be happy because two months ago it wasn't as if the pandemic was over. But I still wear the mask and continue to take care of myself. Once again I feel insecure when I see the weather forecast and they announce the floods in different parts of the United States and the world. I see that man with his scientific and other advances can do nothing against nature. I see it here on television. I also saw it in Argentina less than a year ago. Perhaps it would not have caused me any sadness or concern to see on a newscast in Argentina some crocodiles trying to escape from a fire. They were walking along a road and I was terribly afraid. But fire had already devastated many natural phenomena and there were similar disasters everywhere. I saw it there, I have seen it here too. Television and the media show at the same instant what is happening where we are. This shows that the brain of the world sometimes does as much good as bad.

It was in February, when Argentina was in the middle of summer and I came back from there. As sometimes happens here too, another news item appears and we go to it without worrying about how bad the previous situation was. That has made humans more unpunished in living in a world where bad runs along with goodness. In a few hours we can hear about an act of charity where someone risks their life to save another person and in the same newscast they show a woman who was shot while walking down the street. Sometimes we feel so good when a dog was injured trying to save its owner from someone who broke into the house to steal and thanks to the dog they were both saved. I don't know, I think that, if we put everything in the balance, we would say that there are many bad people, but sometimes the one who does evil receives hate or, vice versa, the good one enjoys a good act. Also sometimes, although in lesser numbers, the bad becomes good. But there is more chance of triumph for the good if he remains good.

CHAPTER 7

In vain I have tried to keep on deluding myself that we can now claim victory and say that those who were lucky enough not to have been infected by COVID-19 are now free to resume their normal rhythm of life. Although I doubt that for many that will be possible. For me, it was lost time that I don't think I can ever get back. At first I stopped doing a lot of things and stayed at home without going out. When I did I realized that my freedom was gone and little by little I became more enclosed in my solitude. But while I thought that what I was going through wouldn't last long I didn't feel so lonely. At first I found it hard to get used to the weekends.

For a long time, my sister Silvia, who works in the Philadelphia suburbs, came to see me every weekend. But then I started not seeing her. I knew I wasn't going to convince her and I was afraid that if she got it, it would be my fault. When I think about it, the months went by fast. But when January came, the month I always go to visit my family, I felt such an emptiness that I was afraid my life would never be the same again. As I said, the years when I had to leave home and live with my relatives to go to school came back to my memory. At that time it was worse. The days seemed to last an eternity. I remembered some passages when my mom came once a month to see us. At least something broke the monotony, especially when my mother stayed more than a day at grandma's house. But now everything was different and when I saw that January had already arrived, I still did not dare to travel because of several fears, one that I would catch it on the trip, another that someone in my family would be infected and I would not be allowed to see him.

A year went by and I don't know how I didn't go crazy during that time. I watched the days go by, my plans were truncated and my life was very monotonous. But I never resigned myself to break all the rules I had imposed on myself until the day came to go and as I already told in another chapter the problems I had to overcome to get there safe and sound. Because just when I decided to go, they imposed more difficult rules for traveling. I don't know how many people told me not to travel. But that's all behind me now.

Now I want to tell what I have been through these five months since I returned to Philadelphia. I thank God that I am still fighting and taking care of myself as much as possible not to get infected. But since I have overdone it in taking care of myself, maybe I will be able to forgive myself if I get the virus and at the same time infect someone else because I will think that I took the best care of myself and I won't be able to reproach myself for having fallen. Thinking about it, how many times I had a cold or a stomach ache because I ate something that made me sick. But how nice it was if I had been told, "That's what you get for eating something you knew was going to make you sick." The first step I've taken to get back to my pre-pandemic life makes me think that nothing will ever be the same again. But now they have started to name a new virus, which I think was already making itself known in other countries, and from what I heard it is called *Monkeypox* in English and Monkeypox in some Spanish speaking countries.   When I have not heard of it for more than a year, I see it again appearing in the news. And maybe it's because I already know I can't avoid him, I will continue to do my best to stay away from him. On TV they show it as something that can leave a mark on your skin, like chicken pox or smallpox and other diseases I heard about when I was a child.

Not only can we talk about the contagion of diseases, but also the newscasts do not stop announcing the crime for the freedom that every citizen has, the right to bear arms. I will repeat ad nauseam, if the right to bear arms is in the constitution that was declared so many years ago, those were other times. It makes you think that no one is going to buy a gun just to scare someone else. The number of victims who are not frightened has not decreased either, nor has the fact of knowing that the number of video cameras and the technique to detect criminals has increased. Nor has the chinstrap used to protect against the virus helped to stop the offender who seems to be afraid of nothing. There is no right for that to happen. It seems that every night they kill just for the sake of killing. We see on more than one occasion in the news someone killing without looking at whom and it is no longer to take the wallet of a poor old lady or for stealing.

What has also changed is how brutal the storms are. There have always been storms. But now they seem to be more destructive and you also hear more about the mess fires make. I heard one person talking about the wars. I wonder if human beings thought that if all that money they spend on war was used for the benefit of mankind how beautiful everything would be. If the money they spend on weapons were used so that every human being could live a life of good health. That is the cruelest thing about human beings. I understand that at the time when I was just a few years old, in my country military service was compulsory. If he was lucky, the soldier would go for a year and come back full of adventures telling about his life in the barracks. But if he had to go to fight, because he was from a country that was at war, most likely he would not return. How many mothers, relatives, girlfriends remembered the day they said goodbye to a young man without knowing that this would be the last day they would see each other. And don't tell me that there is an excuse to force a human being who is still young to kill. Just because in that country they decided to fix things without looking or trying to fix whatever the problem was without spending so much money or taking so many lives.

When there was no television, many things happened without

many people knowing about it, but now for me it was sad to see people in a state in which it was so difficult for the sick person or for their loved ones. At the beginning of the pandemic they showed it more, then we started to not see so many people infected. I think a lot of children didn't get infected or there was little talk about them at the beginning. It seemed more like the ones who were more at risk were the elderly. But it didn't take that long to show that the virus was no respecter of age or social status. We were all prone to fall into the clutches of a new virus where no one can avoid it if they catch it. We don't know if we have eliminated it for good or if it will come back. But I feel we are not out of the woods yet. I pray it goes away soon so I can get back to my old life and can stop thinking about whether I can still feel safe with four vaccines. I will try to continue to take care of myself within the normal. Because I could never forgive myself if by doing as a very Spanish saying goes "no hay que tirar la capa antes de que salga el toro."

I can't help but ignore what is going on worldwide. Thanks to the fact that I have a very large family in some parts of this world in which I live and that makes me think that maybe I was a little exaggerated in isolating myself from everyone. I think I exaggerated too much but I know that I was not the only one and that there were also people who had to go out of the rule and faced the danger of getting infected because there was no other way to go.

Today is a beautiful day, I have the computer in my room and I am enjoying the fresh air coming through the window. Everything seems divine to me and I am full of hope that everything will return to the way it was. I can't say what I will do tomorrow because I don't want to

We have to think so much about the situation we are going through. What we do know is that inflation is giving us signs that it can go down or up as it pleases. Many say that they do not think it will be easy to return to the rhythm of life of more than two years ago. Although they have sacrificed not to travel as they were used to, there are those who still fear that we cannot yet claim victory.

The pandemic does not seem to be ready to leave us yet. Many have not taken vacations as they used to. Others were out of work, lost family members or spent a lot in hospitals. Also because everyone believed that what they had to go through was not going to happen because we were not prepared to be out of work or did not have as much saved to survive what was an unexpected crisis. Many did not believe it would be so difficult to get vaccinated. Others received money from the government and did not work for a certain period of time. I'm not just talking about here because it was and still is something that is alive all over the world. We don't know if there will be another pandemic or we will suffer from another cause. But as the saying goes, "Paradise is not on this earth."

I think we still don't know what the new virus will be like, which is already slowly arriving. Some are still unaware of it and we do not know how it will develop. Because we don't talk about how many have already had it. The world is more interested in other problems like the war in Ukraine… the problems that other countries have with corrupt presidents or the lack of vaccines in certain countries. It is important that COVID is exterminated worldwide so that we can feel safe to claim victory. I have a lot on my brain and I have a hard time remembering what I hear. As I said in part of what I am writing, I did not pay much attention when I got the news that spread and many knew what was going on, but I did not think it would be as serious as it still is. Besides, better not to think about the inflation that is coming. Maybe many have money saved because they didn't spend it traveling or dining out. But COVID kept many from going on vacation or spending less because by staying cooped up they were not tempted to buy as much. This will mean that when we go back to life as it was, we will have learned to live and not be so impatient. We will see how not to rush, but also not to ignore how important it is to follow orders when we are in another case just like it. It is said that the vaccine took a while to reach the public. I remember that I felt desperate because it took me a long time to find the place to get vaccinated. That made me feel desperate. After the first vaccination it was easier. But I still couldn't bring myself to be in public and I have only gone back to the Senior Center because I couldn't stand to be alone anymore.

On my return to the place where I was exercising, I was surprised to see that many of the people I met there looked older. No one wanted to tell me anything about what we were still going through. I was also surprised to see that they were not wearing their chinstraps. Only one had one. When I pointed it out to her she told me that she didn't want to take it off yet. But after a few weeks she took it off. So did I. I don't know if it's the time I go or what's going on, but I don't see as many people as before, when it used to be crowded all the time. Nobody looked the same. It seems to me that many of us are missing, but I also see people who weren't there before, although they are few.

I still have a long way to go to get back to my old life. I must say that I considered myself a healthy person until two years ago. But suddenly I find that I am not well. Whenever I went to the doctor, nothing was found. He recommended me to have some tests once a year, but they were always the same. He said I just had a little arthritis. It just attacked me when I least wanted it and it has attacked me hard. But I will get strong enough to overcome it and I hope I find the solution quickly. Because I've been two years waiting for this pandemic time to end so I can go back to being the full of life person I always was. But let it be soon. So I can say "goodbye to the pandemic."

For me, the pandemic complicated my life. Many plans I had fell apart. And when I got into a state where I felt overwhelmed I started to let myself be and now I think that the two years I spent without being able to go on with my life made me feel bad, not physically but mentally, I can even say that I got sick. My arthritis became chronic. I had trouble going to the doctor. I always went once a year and had all the necessary tests. The doctor would tell me I just had a little arthritis. I thought the pain in my left leg was just because I wasn't exercising. Or maybe it just wasn't easy at first to get used to being inactive, with no schedule to keep, trying to kill time, reading or glued to the TV to distract myself. But I couldn't find anything I liked.

I was curious to watch the few programs I watched when I arrived in this country, but they did not distract me at all. There were the ones about the Wild West, the cowboys as we called them in Argentina when we were kids. I thought I was going to like them as I did at the beginning. But I quickly realized that in westerns, as we called that kind of movies, there was also a lot of blood. Also, the police movies left a lot to be desired. When I saw them again they no longer held the interest I felt when I saw them the first time, although I admired the scenery they had. They reminded me a little of my childhood when I lived in the country: the harnesses. At home these were sheep. In the movies they were more like cows. Sometimes they would show something about Indians. But I didn't like it because they all looked like bullies and they had severe features. I stayed with some comic programs that sometimes they show us again and they are not so dramatic.

But loneliness has turned me into a different person. That and my health, which, although I managed to save on several occasions, have made me a little more aggressive. Sometimes in the loneliness I live in I see that I have changed. I get angry easily. I get bored. I see that I am getting old and that makes me a little grotesque. I have no patience for certain things and I am afraid that I will become a grumpy old woman. No patience for anything. I have changed and I don't feel like a confident person. I feel less and less like I was and I'm scared to have to talk because, even though I try to pretend that sometimes I'm talking, I suddenly don't remember something and that humiliates me a bit. But now that I was starting to feel confident again I see that I can't pretend anymore. But I always find people who help me and I can get out of trouble when in the middle of a conversation I feel that my mind stops working and I feel sorry for myself. I feel worse when someone wants to correct me or notices me because most of the people who are close to me are around the same age as me, I can manage to fake my mistake and add to the narration something. And especially sometimes the relatives are the ones who make me feel worse and I fall into hours of insecurity. I also sometimes think that this didn't happen to me for a long time when I was shooting the pandemic by counting the days that seemed to have gone by without catching it.

    I stopped doing what I had been doing for many more than a year, I have been away from the few friends I have left. I don't remember hearing or seeing that from my grandmothers and older relatives because at that time human beings didn't live that long. I had better learn to live in the moment. No more daydreaming. Better that I let my destiny take its course. In the future I will try not to be so selfish. But what I ask God most of all is that I not be so ambitious. To be content with what I have. That I let my destiny take its course. That doesn't mean I won't do anything. I still have some dreams to fulfill, but I will not let them complicate my existence. I will also do one thing at a time. That way, if I don't achieve what I want, I won't feel so strongly the failure of many setbacks. But I will suffer only for one misfortune. But I would like to leave this world where I will be remembered for something good I have done wshile I was on this planet.

    Going back to the pandemic, I will never forget that it was at that time that I lost a good friend. Zulema was not my blood relative, but she was as if she was. We would always stop at her house when we traveled to Argentina. And she always welcomed us with open arms. Her house was her house and mine. We always had memories of the crazy things we did. Anecdotes that I will never forget. Our stay in her house left traces that last. I always had the funniest things happen with her. Not because I was a clown, but I never stopped telling her what I was doing. And she would turn everything I told her into a funny story and we laughed non-stop. Luis, Zulema's husband, had to make us shut up because we couldn't stop laughing until he put his foot down and made us shut up. The truth is that we were unconscious for having such a chat and not letting him sleep. Zulema was a fighter and managed, after studying, to open a hairdresser's shop in Puente Saavedra, Buenos Aires. After Luis passed away, she came to Bariloche and bought a house where she planned to spend the rest of her life. Whenever I went to see my family I stayed with her for at least two nights or more. And we always relived the good times we had. But the last time I went I saw her sad. I thought that she, like so many people, had lost the good mood she always had because of the pandemic. She did not want me to stay at least one night with her. She dismissed me saying that we would be together when the virus was exterminated. I returned to the United States thinking about going back and reliving the good times we had had together for so long. I said goodbye imagining my return and wished that time would pass quickly.

I will also always remember that I lost a great friend whose name was Marta and with her I also lived many adventures. With her I learned to dance Argentine folklore and we had some adventures.

good and bad performances representing our homeland. No one ever praised me, but I did the best I could. And our friendship continued until after she fought so hard, death overcame her. For me it was something that left me bad. I cried angrily at first and then it seemed wrong to do so and I calmed down. What hurt me the most was not being by her side when she was leaving for good. All I do now is pray for her and strive to believe that there is a place in heaven full of flowers because she loved them so much.

I have the illusion that she will be with her mother in a paradise where there is no more suffering and God will have them there eternally. How nice it would be if it were like that and that we would all find ourselves there one day with our loved ones. But when I said it, those who were suspicious feared that by thinking about death one could call it and make it come sooner. Many preferred not to think or talk about something that will happen to all of us. There are also those who think it is better not to ruin their lives by torturing themselves imagining what the final day will be like. Others think and fear more to suffer from illness and long life. There are those who live for the moment and don't waste time trying to imagine what that last day will be like and live happily. I try to behave myself.

Because I don't want to waste my life without having to enjoy being as good as I can. I think I think that way because I like to be thought of as a good person. No one died and came back to earth to tell the tale. In the meantime, we are still struggling with the viruses that continue to worry us. We are very close to more than two years into the pandemic. Many have already taken the necessary vaccines against the virus and I have not heard any more about *Monkeypox*. I hope it will go down in history without causing as many deaths as the CORONA virus did. Which I don't think I was the only person who mentally followed in its footsteps. But you never know, maybe we will continue to be visited by many more viruses.

Talking about the last few years where we have been vaccinated as a precaution for several viruses that passed and we were scared thinking that they were going to wreak more havoc, we were visited by them and they passed without stopping, some still exist, but they have stopped causing fear. So far there has been no more talk of *Monkeypox*. If it arrives, perhaps we will be more forewarned and we will know how to protect ourselves more. We will no longer be afraid of them. But there is no certainty that we will be free of new contagions. Just as we are seeing that in our planet several terrestrial phenomena are happening that make us think that something is happening and many die in fires, earthquakes, floods or many other accidents. I believe that there is no country that has not suffered from some plague or natural accidents lately. At this moment we only wish that all the bad things come to an end, that human beings become more humane. And even if we do not want to try to take care of ourselves more, let us not stop taking precautions for the good of humanity.

www.ingramcontent.com/pod-product-compliance
Lightning Source LLC
LaVergne TN
LVHW041545060526
838200LV00037B/1151